82

6-

THE KING PENGUIN BOOKS
40
EDWARD GORDON CRAIG

EDWARD GORDON CRAIG PRACTISED SEVERAL CRAFTS · 1889 TO 97 WAS ACTOR · 1893 TO 1926 WAS METTEUR-EN-SCÈNE I.E. PRODUCED PLAYS AND OPERAS WAS DESIGNER OF SCENES AND COSTUMES · AND WAS WOOD EN-GRAVER · COMPOSED SOME TUNES · WROTE SOME BOOKS · MADE SOME ETCHINGS 1906 TO 12

EGC · ROME · 1919

EDWARD
GORDON CRAIG

DESIGNS
FOR THE THEATRE

━━

JANET LEEPER

PENGUIN BOOKS

THE KING PENGUIN BOOKS

Editor: N.B.L.Pevsner
Technical Editor: R.B. Fishenden

*

Published by Penguin Books, Limited,
Harmondsworth, Middlesex, England, and by
Penguin Books Pty., Ltd., 200, Normanby Road
Melbourne, Australia

*

This volume published 1948
Made in Great Britain

*

Text printed by R.&R.Clark, Ltd, Edinburgh.
Plates made and printed by John Swain & Son Ltd,
Barnet. Cover by William Grimmond after
a design of Edward Gordon Craig.

T was as an actor that Gordon Craig approached the whole problem of the Theatre. This is too often forgotten. Considering his later fame, it is as well to remember that for eight years he was a member of Irving's company at the Lyceum (1889–97) struggling with all the others to emulate Irving and in doing so refusing to use the rich natural gifts with which his mother, Ellen Terry, had dowered him. For Irving's style, 'wonderful mosaics of bits of acting thought out touch by touch', was a vehicle for his own extraordinary talents, but useless as a model for others to follow.

In the summer vacations from the Lyceum, Craig had played some thirty or forty parts, ranging from farce to leading Shakespearean roles, before he turned seriously to production. Hamlet he had first tackled in September 1894, at Hereford, when he was twenty-two, playing Romeo for the first time on the previous night, and thereafter he played Hamlet whenever he got the chance. In 1897, owing to the sudden illness of Nutcombe Gould, he was called on to play the part for the last six performances of the season with the Ben Greet Company at the Olympic Theatre, Westminster. 'Can you play Hamlet to-night?' wired Greet, and Craig, asking for the necessary permission from Irving, got the apt reply, 'The readiness is all'. His performance is remembered with delight by those who were fortunate enough to see it. He had all the gifts: voice, presence, intelligence, something of his mother's radiance and grace of movement, and the inherited talent for acting natural to one born in the theatrical purple who had been perfectly at home on the stage since earliest boyhood.

Bernard Shaw, with his usual acumen, was quick to see in him a young actor who would be useful for his new comedy, *You*

Never Can Tell; but Craig was busy playing Hamlet elsewhere and was not to be drawn aside. At this time he was not thinking of stage management at all, but only of acting. A while later Granville Barker tried to lure him into the Frohman, Barker, Barrie, Shaw group, as actor ... 'nothing doing'.

His talent for designing was hardly yet manifest, but he lost no opportunity of trying to draw, wherever he might be. He went to no School of Art. He picked up the first essentials of wood-cutting from a painter, and after some six or eight years this was to become more than a hobby – even bringing him a precarious livelihood when the stage could hold him no more. His first essay in stage production had taken place as early as December 1893, in Uxbridge – an adaptation of de Musset's *On ne badine pas avec l'amour*, in which he acted the chief part of Perdican.

In 1897 he ceased to act, he who had it all in him. Ellen Terry never ceased to lament this. 'I have never known anyone with so much natural gift for the stage', she wrote. 'Unconsciously he did everything right – I mean all the technical things over which some of us have to labour for years. ... I have good reason to be proud of what he has done since, but I regret the lost actor *always*.'

Already Craig had the unhappy feeling that the stage was not what it could some day be; but it was only in 1906–9 that he saw that the theatre must be changed from top to bottom if it was to be worthy of its great tradition. No one else dared see that. A revolution was necessary. How to bring it about? But we will come to that presently. In 1897–9 he did not know what it was that had to be done; but his immediate course was clear. He threw up 'eight pounds a week for nothing a month', except for what he could earn by drawing for journals and newspapers – rather than give in. Henceforth he worked unceasingly in every way that lay open to him – and there were many – to make his vision a reality, but never again at the beck and call of any 'managements'.

First came the London productions, the first four with his friend Martin Shaw, the composer.

1900 Purcell's opera *Dido and Aeneas* given by the Purcell Operatic Society at Hampstead.

1901 *The Masque of Love* (from Purcell's *Dioclesian*) and a revival of *Dido and Aeneas* at the Coronet Theatre, Notting Hill Gate, again with Martin Shaw.

1902 Handel's *Acis and Galatea* and a revival of *The Masque of Love* at the Great Queen Street Theatre, with Martin Shaw.
Laurence Housman's *Bethlehem* at the Imperial Institute, South Kensington, and part of the production (*i.e.* three scenes) of Roze's *Sword and Song* at the Shaftesbury Theatre.

1903 Ibsen's *The Vikings at Helgeland* and Shakespeare's *Much Ado about Nothing* for Ellen Terry at the Imperial Theatre.

Those who saw these productions remember them with wonder. W.B. Yeats writes in his *Ideas of Good and Evil* of 'Gordon Craig's purple backcloth that made Dido and Aeneas seem wandering on the edge of eternity', and Henry Nevinson, who was present at the Coronet Theatre, wrote in his note-book: 'Both *Dido* (which the people *would* call Dodo) and *The Masque* went gloriously. Great beauty of the purples and greys and greens in the *Dido* against the vast background of purple eternity. The music was lovely throughout but richer and fuller of possibility in *The Masque*. Daring colours and arrangements. White figures and greys and greens, with but rare touches of red, the more brilliant for their variety.'

Count Kessler, who was later to commission the Cranach Press *Hamlet*, some illustrations from which are to be found in this book, writing long after described his impressions of the plays at the Imperial Theatre thus:

It must have been about 1900 (1903) when the first stage scenes that he created for his mother, Ellen Terry, astounded London by their almost fanatical simplification and their turning away from realism. While the Meiningen Company and, in England, Beerbohm Tree were making the stage into a branch of the Arts and Crafts Museum, piling up accurate historical detail, people found that Craig had used for Ibsen's *The Vikings* only curtains as background, and only such properties as were indispensable to the action; and in the church scene in *Much Ado about Nothing*, except for the curtains there was only one strong ray of sunlight, falling on the stage in a thousand colours through an invisible stained-glass window.

What Count Kessler saw was a single shaft of light falling on a huge cross hanging from above, lighting up its many colours little by little. Gradually the beam widened so that more and more light filled the stage, the figures in the foreground remaining shrouded in darkness. The curtains on either side were painted with pillars and hung in folds. It was all very simple and severe – an antithesis to the gorgeous setting Irving had used not long before.

In point of fact, *The Vikings* had a great deal more to it than curtains. There was a most solid structure of rocks and cliffs down which the actors had to clamber and in one scene a great platform. But gone were the old flies and wings and borders with a painted backcloth up-stage; footlights were reduced to a minimum and the light fell from above; and the costumes were planned as an artist would plan them – as part of his picture, and not for their individual effect. This, in itself alone, was a tremendous innovation. Colour was used in combination with the movement on the stage, and we already see here – in 1900–3 – the beginning of what was to lead to Diaghilev's Russian Ballet. For

8

Craig's theatre was always most musical, most poetic. To achieve a certain effect he used dresses, in *The Vikings*, of eight shades of grey – he has always loved greys and browns, very low in tone; besides these, great semi-circular cloaks, all of clear colour – a blaze of it. There were also golden ornaments of delicate intricacy, trimmings in rope, and studded shields of bold and simple design, some of which, being beautiful and serviceable, have survived to this day. *The Times* wrote that the scenic simplicity and severity were impressive, 'harmonious in colouring, broad and massive in design'.

For Laurence Housman's *Bethlehem* Craig dressed his shepherds in hessian, a material not used as yet as he used it in the theatre, and in the strong light, covered the stage with sacks and hurdles, representing flocks of sheep, achieving thus a homogeneous picture, far from reality or preciousness. This was in 1902, remember. What Craig did in 1902, Reinhardt had not begun to dream of doing.

Very few designs are to be found of these early productions, but there is in this book a young shepherd from *Bethlehem* (Plate 1) and the rush-dress man in *Acis and Galatea* (Plate 2), and a photograph of the performance of *Bethlehem* at the Imperial Institute (Plate 7); and sometimes a scene or a costume was made into a woodcut, as for instance the sorceress in *Dido and Aeneas* (page 11), or the cloud backcloth for the same opera (Plate 6) or the scene of the fight between Arnolf and Sigurd in *The Vikings* (Plate 9).

Another woodcut which dates from these early years of the century is of the curious forest of trees, built in the round, in *Sword and Song* (Plate 8). This rose from a hillock which covered the entire stage, the prototype of that later woodland scene in Granville Barker's production of *A Midsummer Night's Dream* (1914).

9

To regard Craig as a man who went in for elaborate scenery is a misconception. He simplified and got away from all the extravagant staging of his time, so that the theatrical element might be freed from its shackles. He is above all an original man. He does things his own way and they are not anybody else's way. So it came about that there were plenty of people to criticize his productions. Of the performance of *Acis and Galatea* and *The Masque of Love* we read that 'the dresses bore as little resemblance to the actual costume of any period or latitude as the scenes did to anything to be observed in Sicily or elsewhere'. In other words, they were original inventions of the poetic fancy.

Contrary to what might be supposed by those who only know Craig's later work with its feeling for height, he had lowered the proscenium arch for the performances at the Hampstead Conservatoire (now the Embassy Theatre), making a long rectangular opening for his stage picture, and with this new shape he was able to sweep away the footlights and light his scenes from above. Martin Shaw was in charge of the music, and the music was wedded to the movement and the movement to the lighting in a harmonious whole. Some of this movement is communicated to us in his working drawings.

There is something to be learnt from notices written at the time. The clouds of misconception had not yet risen, obscuring the view. Craig wanted a serious theatre and not a theatre of compromise, playing down to the tastes of the time which demanded ever more and more elaborate staging, a theatre in fetters to get-rich-quick managements; but he found his countrymen content with their chains and unwilling to shake them off or to accept the message he brought. *The Vikings*, with Ellen Terry playing the leading part, was an artistic success and a financial failure, and

THE SORCERESS · DIDO AND ÆNEAS · WOODCUT · 1900

II

Much Ado about Nothing did not retrieve her fortunes. In April the theatre had opened and in June the theatre was shut. No support, either public or private, had come, and unless the artist is supported how can he do his work?

They order these matters better abroad, where every artist is acknowledged as a useful member of the community with a necessary part to play, and in Central Europe, Scandinavia and Russia, and indeed all over the Continent, there are well-established municipal and state theatres running a repertory system as a necessary part of civic life. So it is perhaps not surprising that it was on the Continent that Craig's ideas took root and that his work flourished and has had its greatest influence far from his native land.

In July 1904, Craig, who was living in a little studio in London, writing mimo-dramas and masques (Plates 3 and 5) with no prospect of producing them, suddenly received an invitation from Dr Brahm of the Lessing Theater to go to Germany to produce Hofmannsthal's version of Otway's *Venice Preserved*, and in August he set out for Berlin. At Weimar he first met Count Kessler, who immediately commissioned five wood-engravings to illustrate Hofmannsthal's play *The White Fan*, to be published by the Insel Verlag. Here at last was quick encouragement, here was work! This was the beginning of Craig's long association with Kessler, a description of whom he has given in *Woodcuts and Some Words*:

> He was a stranger, one who liked good books, good printing, and liked them new. To him, while old books of the 13th and 3rd century were good, books of the day were even better ... All the time he went unceasingly here and there, placing sums of money in one branch of art after another. Wood engraving – Painting – the Stage –

Publishing – Printing – Type-cutting – Paper-making – Literature – Sculpture – Music – there was nothing in the Arts that he missed. He braced up all these things by the sole means in his power, not by little occasional bursts of anxious sympathy and dabbling in them himself, but by a trim personal attention given to seeing them braced up. For him I made, in 1905, these five wood blocks, four of which were published by the Insel Verlag in Leipzig in 1907.

The year 1905 marks the establishment of Craig's renown in Europe. Exhibitions of his work were held all over Germany and in Vienna. While making designs for *Venice Preserved*, which was produced at the Lessing Theater (Plates 10 and 11), Eleonora Duse wrote to Craig from Italy commissioning designs for a production of *Electra*, and these were executed under his supervision by the scene painter Impekoven and a costumier in Berlin and were despatched to her in Italy. For himself he made the drawing reproduced in this book (Plate 4).

Time has not aged the wonder of this design nor of those he made for Duse, which in their noble simplicity and calm beauty seem to express what the designers of to-day are still searching for. Yet they were never used by Duse, perhaps because she was herself frustrated by uninspired managements. Meeting Craig a year later, she invited him to Italy to supervise the production of Ibsen's *Rosmersholm* at the Teatro della Pergola in Florence. He painted for her a scene in deep indigo with two great openings, used alternatively, through one of which was seen the avenue of a park, through the other a long staircase. The beauty of the setting lay, as in so many of Craig's designs, in its simplicity and just proportion, and at the first night the great actor Salvini who was sitting in the stalls was heard to exclaim as the curtain rose: 'Bella! Bella!'

When later on Duse wished to give a performance of the play in Nice, Craig's scene was ruthlessly cut down by the management, who fitted it into the smaller theatre by chopping a couple of feet off here and there, completely destroying its proportions. When Craig protested against such treatment of his scene, Duse responded with a brief note: 'What they have done to your scene they have been doing for years to my art'. Which is hardly a reply.

*

Craig's little booklet, *The Art of the Theatre*, published in 1905, in which he had formulated his ideas for the first time, had been a protest against just such happenings. It is written in the form of a Dialogue between a Director and a Playgoer. 'His fundamental position is no doubt unassailable', wrote *The Times* of this. Craig argued that when three or four people are in charge of a performance in the theatre, no visual unity, no harmony of movement, lighting and colour with action, music and speech, to produce a supreme *theatrical* effect, is possible. His first plea had been for unity of production under one man – and this was the practical actor speaking out of his own experience. His next was that there should be some recognition of the fact that there *was* such a thing as an 'Art of the Theatre'. Literature, painting, music, he said, had their standards. The theatre had none. It lived from hand to mouth or from season to season, at the mercy of the whims of theatrical promoters following ephemeral fashions or the personal ambitions or predilections of actor-managers. He pleaded for a School, where the art of the theatre might be studied in all its aspects. Such logic, resting on broad principles, was unimpeachable. The statement is still to-day the clearest and best exposition of the fundamental problems of the theatre.

14

If people in England had been slow to receive Craig's ideas, those abroad were not so slow. The actor Max Reinhardt, who had been working under Brahm at the Deutsches Theater, and had been producing plays on his own account since 1902 at the Kleines Theater in Berlin, seized on them with avidity. When Craig's book appeared, he had just taken over the direction of the Deutsches Theater from Brahm, and a significant change now came over the productions there. He began to make use of the gold-mine of Craig's original theories and to exploit them to the full. His so-called realistic presentation of poetic drama now gave way to symbolic and decorative treatment such as we associate with the modern theatre in Germany, with beautiful lighting such as Craig had already shown in his London productions. Led by the enthusiasm and practical energy of Count Kessler, the public flocked to Reinhardt's theatre and the success of the new move-ment was assured. From Reinhardt it was ultimately to spread to the whole German-speaking stage, so that a 'Craigische Vor-stellung' became an accepted expression for a performance on the lines advocated by Craig, and added an adjective to the German language.

*

Whence had come these scenes which foreshadowed a new era? In his search for first principles Craig had gone back to the very basis of all theatrical design: the human figure in relation to its environment, the three-dimensional 'place' rather than the two-dimensional 'scene'. One of his early designs for *Hamlet*, made in 1896, already shows those vast walls, those inky shadows, that blare of light at just the spot where Bernardo is so dramatically to appear. He says that a series of drawings of the Roman Theatre at Orange in *Harper's Monthly Magazine* in 1895 excited his interest and showed him the dramatic possibilities of large open-ings and deep shadows. With its huge doors and air of mystery it conjured up memories of Hampton Court Palace and the im-mense four-poster beds there, 'with slim towering posts wrapped in damask and curtains falling from high up, and a bunch of plumes at each top corner', which he had seen as a child when living in a cottage in the vicinity. There are several references to Hampton Court in his note-book, and in 1903 when he produced some scenes in the music-drama *Sword and Song* for his uncle, Fred Terry, comes the entry: 'Then came the first of the Tall Beds seen so often at Hampton Court'. There is something symbolic in the fact that the latent decorative sense of the future Royal De-signer should have been first awakened by the domestic furnish-ings of a building so deeply rooted in English history.

Another and greater influence was that of the two books of *Architettura* (1545) by the old Italian master, Serlio, which he had bought in London in 1903. Later, when he founded his journal *The Mask*, he published in its first number Serlio's historically important account of the Tragic, Comic and Satyric (pastoral) scenes for the Renaissance theatre in Italy, with the original wood-cuts, translated for the first time into English. But it was not Serlio's *Second Book*, which deals with perspective in the theatre, which enthralled him most – it was the *First Book*, with its geo-metrical diagrams:

These diagrams held me in 1904 or whenever it was (he wrote to a friend in 1946), and today as I sit here the same book again holds me – only that. I look at it and endless thoughts are born within a few moments ... I would not like any young fellow of tomorrow to labour to read Serlio's *words*, for I am inclined to believe the young fellow of tomorrow will do as I did and do – look on to and in to the diagrams

16

and 'seek to know no more'. Then these seeming dead lines of those old cuts will come to life for him as they came to life for me.

At the turn of the century, the would-be reformers of the theatre were few, and they were largely unknown to one another. The Swiss, Adolphe Appia, who had approached staging and decoration in the theatre through the study of Wagner's music-dramas and whose aims were in many ways similar to Craig's, was unknown to Craig until the spring of 1914, when an Exhibition of Theatrical Designs in Zürich revealed the work of each to the other. Isadora Duncan, the American dancer who was to have such a profound influence on European art, came to Berlin in 1905, and it was there that Craig, attending one of her dance-recitals, immediately recognized in her a genius, bent on the same mission as himself: the creation of what the poet Yeats has called 'The Theatre of Beauty'. Together they roamed over Europe, she dancing, he designing, bringing new courage to those who were turning away from the moribund theatre, the stagey 'realism' and the dead wood of the past. In 1906 Craig published a portfolio, *Isadora Duncan: Six Movement Designs*, with the Insel Verlag in Leipzig, with a poem to his enchantress, who had also enchanted everyone else. Her first visit to Russia, in January 1905, is recalled by both Stanislavsky and Fokine as of enormous significance to the development of theatrical art in Russia, and especially of the Diaghilev Ballet, which was formed three years later – though neither of them in their published work remembers how early she went there.

Craig's *Studies for Movement* and his series *The Steps* belong to this time :

> Among all the dreams that the architect has laid upon the earth, I know of no more lovely things than his flights of steps leading up and

17

leading down, and of this feeling about architecture in my art I have often thought how one could give life (not a voice) to these places, using them to a dramatic end. When this desire came to me I was continually designing dramas wherein the place was architectural and lent itself to my desire. And so I began with a drama called *The Steps*.

Jessner was to raise a whole school of production on this one idea, while *Wapping Old Stairs* (Plate 5), with its vast palisades, has clearly inspired some of Walt Disney's best imaginative work for the films.

In 1906–7 Craig planned a ballet on the subject of *Psyche*, a project which was later brought by Count Kessler before Diaghilev, who for once found the ideas contained in it too daring for his acceptance. By nature Craig, with his feeling for rhythmic movement and intense love of music, is an ideal choreographic designer and maker of ballets. A few drawings leave us to infer what he had in mind (Plate 12). In all these matters one is struck with the amazing richness of Craig's contribution. It was not limited to any one direction but seemed to be an outpouring of every kind at one and the same time.

*

In the midst of all this Craig made an extraordinary discovery. Like all real discoveries it is difficult to evaluate correctly or to write about. This was that there was a 'dramatic principle' in nature – something akin to music or architecture. To demonstrate this principle he built a working model of screens which changed and unfolded before the eyes of the spectators, a Scene which was dramatic *in itself*. In this there were no coloured surfaces, all was done by light. Form, movement, colour – these three.

The relation of light to this scene is akin to that of the sun on the leaves, the moon on the river or seas, to that of the bow to the violin or of the pen to paper. For the light *travels* over the scene – it does not stay in one fixed place ... travelling, it produces the music.

An account of the working of the 'Scene for the Poetic Drama' has come down to us from a notable observer, Filiberto Scarpelli, the Florentine artist-architect-writer, in a letter to his friend Giovanni Grasso, the Sicilian actor, who had asked for a report.

My impression? Craig is a prodigious man, if prodigious signi-fies the power of conjuring up from nothing, before your eyes, that which amazes you. And the elements of which Craig makes use for his creations are nothing or almost nothing: some screens and some electric lights. He sets upon the stage of his little theatre (no bigger than a marionette theatre) his small screens, and, while you look on, with a rapid movement of the hand arranges them in a certain way; a ray of electric light comes to strike between those simple rectangles of cardboard, and the miracle is accomplished: you behold a majestic scene; the sense of the small disappears absolutely; you forget the dimensions of the theatre, because of the harmonious relationship which Craig knows how to bring about 'twixt the lights and the lines. Another slight movement of the screens (always before your eyes) and the scene changes and then changes again without the lines and the light effects ever recalling to you that which you have already seen. And thus one passes from the vision of a *piazza*, a street, an im-posing portico, to that of a *sala*, a prison, a subterranean dungeon. Craig is a great painter, a great architect, a great poet. He paints with light, he constructs with a few rectangles of cardboard, and with the harmony of his colours and of his lines he creates profound sensations, as only the fathers of poetry knew how to create. I do not exaggerate, dear Giovanni. The sight of some screens for 'Othello' gave me the thrill which only the *reading of Shakespeare* had been able to give me! We are far, very far, from the usual scenographic resources, be they

19

even the best which can be remembered. If one does not see Craig's theatre one cannot imagine what this man knows how to do. ... You have lost a sight which is among the finest which I have witnessed since I was born, not excluding the majestic spectacles of Nature itself.

The etchings of *Scene*, 1906–7, strange precursors of a cubism which had not yet come up over the horizon, were exhibited first in Florence and then in London, but it was not until 1923 that the Oxford Press issued them in book form with a Foreword and four Sonnets by the Poet Laureate, who wrote:

> *Here is the work. Who, greater than his age*
> *Will use this work to consecrate the stage?*

There was no reply; so the work went on, as ever, in Craig's mind and in his studio, but not in the wider arena of the theatre itself – where it belongs.

*

The years 1907–8–9 were Craig's 'special' years, when the bright stream of inspiration bubbled forth apparently inexhaustibly in every direction, taking ever new forms. All who came within his ambit were enriched thereby. To these years belong the magnificent series of designs for *Macbeth* – rejected, to his eternal shame, by Sir Herbert Tree – one of which is to be found in this book (Plate 13): more than a hundred designs cut in boxwood and reproduced in *The Mask* (Plates 14–19); all save one of the etchings in *Scene* (Plates 20 and 21); the designs for *King Lear* and *The Merchant of Venice*; the carving and printing of the first Black Figures (Plates 26, 27, 28) and the founding of *The Mask*.

The project of publishing a journal in which, both by writing and engraving, he could tell others what he had to say then and there had been in Craig's mind for some time. Already he had written and illustrated *The Page*, from 1898 to 1901, engraving about two hundred and thirty boxwood blocks for it. No publisher could be found for a serious journal devoted to the theatre, and one went so far even as to declare that £10,000 would be needed to issue it. Craig thereupon decided to start it himself with a working capital of £5, and in March 1908, Vol. I, No. 1 of *The Mask* appeared. A thin monthly, of foolscap size, admirably printed in Florence in thick black type on hand-made paper with green covers, it was richly illustrated with beautiful woodcuts, ancient and modern, and was a rare money's-worth at a shilling. The magazine throve and was soon printing 10,000 copies a month. Odd numbers that come to light nowadays find ready buyers. Even the advertisements were good to look at, and the whole journal was so well-informed and stimulating that from its inception it excited widespread interest.

The Mask not only looked into the future, it delved into the past, reprinting many of E. W. Godwin's famous papers on the architecture and costuming of Shakespeare's plays, which had first appeared in the 'seventies, in *The Architect*. As a boy of eleven Craig had seen his father's hand in the staging of *Claudian* at the Princess's Theatre and it is perhaps from Godwin – the brilliant architect, theatrical critic, archaeologist and expert designer of stage settings and costumes – that Craig derives his flair for scholarship, which has made his own researches into theatrical history of such importance. Month by month these were recorded in *The Mask*, which became the first theatrical journal of its time. Articles on the theatre of yesterday or of to-morrow or of the day after to-morrow had the Craig swing and the Craig ring. Some-

times he wrote *in propria persona*, but dozens of pseudonyms mysti-
fied the unwary; when they thought they were reading the distilled
wisdom of half a dozen European savants, they were often enjoying a one-man show.

One article, 'The Actor and the Über-Marionette', written in
1906, which was later incorporated in *On the Art of the Theatre*
(1911), calls for comment. Storms raged round this inspired pro-
nouncement which has hung like a banner from Craig's castle
walls ever since. He was accused of wanting to sweep away the
whole tribe of actors and actresses in order to put inhuman puppets in their place. At the head of his article he had quoted
Eleonora Duse's saying: 'To save the Theatre, the Theatre must
be destroyed, the actors and actresses must all die of the plague. ...
They make art impossible.' Years later he replied to his critics in
a new preface to the 1924 edition of *On the Art of the Theatre*,
which had by then gone into many editions in eight languages:
'I no more want to see the living actors replaced by things of wood
than the great Italian actress of our day wants all the actors to die.
... The Über-Marionette is the actor plus fire, minus egotism: the
fire of the gods and demons, without the smoke and steam of
mortality.'

*

In the early days, when Craig was young and unknown, among
the few who had understood his aim had been the poet W.B.
Yeats. In his little room off the Euston Road, with the blue curtains, Yeats would discourse on the poetic drama in his vivid
magnetic way, peering with myopic eyes into the darkness while
Craig was happy to sit and listen to him. Yeats had longed for
productions of his plays by Craig, and so in 1910, when he and
Lady Gregory had made the Abbey Theatre in Dublin famous

all over the world, Craig gave him a set of screens and made designs for *Deirdre*, *The Hour Glass* and *On Baile's Strand* (Plates 22, 23 and 24). The screens, first used in 1911, proved invaluable and, being easy to handle and capable of being arranged in an endless number of combinations, have been in use ever since. Whether, in strange hands, these screens have ever come to the same vivid life as when guided by their creator – that is another question.

Seeing the Theatre steadily and seeing it whole, Craig could not be expected to descend into the arena and make ignoble bargains with actor-managers out for their own glory; and so it came about that only the Moscow Art Theatre and the Royal Theatre at Copenhagen were patient and understanding enough to employ him on his own terms.

Of the various projects which did not materialize or were frustrated, that of *Macbeth* for Tree at His Majesty's in 1909 was perhaps the greatest loss. The story is told in the memoirs of the scene-painter Joseph Harker, who relates with relish how he managed to persuade Tree to scrap the models prepared by Craig. 'Unhappy Harker', wrote Desmond McCarthy when the book appeared, 'you will be remembered as typical of those sturdy professionals who, alas! not content with that great share of lucrative success which naturally falls to them, but spurred by a curious suspicion of the genuine artist, proceed to wreck even those rare chances which come their way.'

Stanislavsky's invitation to Craig to produce a play at the Moscow Art Theatre was more propitious. Craig set to work to prepare complete models for *Hamlet* (Plate 25), the play and the part which above all others he seemed to have been playing all his life. Many ideas of a novel and penetrating kind were carried out

23

in this production, which took place in January 1912, amid the acclamation of the public and the critics alike. Everyone who saw it remembers the impression it made – it was presented more than four hundred times – and speaks with emotion of an event without parallel in the history of the theatre. But neither Stanislavsky nor Craig was satisfied. Stanislavsky, in his book *My Life in Art*, writes quite frankly of his failure to do justice to Craig and of the thrilling experience he and his assistant Sulerjitsky had in working with Craig, in spite of language and other difficulties. In the theatre Craig is a dynamo of energy and practical understanding, knowing exactly what he wants and determined to get it. Not even a Russian winter could cool his ceaseless activity and enthusiasm. For the Court Scene Craig conceived the idea of a sea of gold, an immense glittering cloak made of cloth-of-gold from the Stanislavsky factory streaming down from the steps where the King and Queen sat. Of this scene Craig writes: 'Under this gold cloak stood two pupils who were later to prove of worth in the theatre of Russia, Vakhtangov and Miss Bierman. The two young people *understood* (perhaps even better than did Stanislavsky) my aims for a Theatre to serve drama greatly, and they were most faithful and remembered and carried on the ideas I gave and thus they became famous and made famous their theatres.' It was Vakhtangov who created the renowned Habimah Company.

A by-product of this presentation of *Hamlet* were the figures carved in thin wood which were used by Craig in his model theatre to explain the many movements of the actors in *Hamlet* to the Russians. Beginning as white figures in a model theatre, they ended up as Black Figures on paper. How describe their metamorphosis? Look at the Poet and his Thought, or Hamlet and his Daemon (Plate 28). He lived in Craig's pocket during

24

rehearsals in Moscow, taking his place in the model theatre when needed. Then one day he was inked and pressed on thin paper, in the same way as woodcuts are inked and impressed on fine papers. Thus were the Black Figures created – half-woodcut, half-marionette, strange creatures of practical use and imagination. A whole series of characters appeared, some belonging to other plays – *The Merchant of Venice* (Plates 26 and 27), *On Baile's Strand*, *Macbeth*, *Beauty and the Beast* – while others took on immortality in Count Kessler's hand-printed edition of *Hamlet*, prepared by the Cranach Press. There you will find (if you can find a copy) the Second Gravedigger with his long spade (Plate 29), the spectral Ghost (Plate 30), the Actor in 'a forest of feathers' with the attributes of his craft (Plate 31), Hamlet greeting the actors (Plates 32 and 33), the Player-King asleep in the orchard (Plate 34) – while the Poisoner approaches from the opposite page across the intervening letterpress to pour poison in his ear, – the Court in confusion and the King calling for lights, as it was not seen even in Moscow (Plate 35). Not all walked abroad in the Russian model theatre, many took shape only as illustrations to the printed book: but from 1912 to 1929, when the German edition appeared, Craig was on and off at work, carving, cutting and printing, so that more than sixty figurines and wood-blocks were added to the dozen or so of the experimental theatre.

Count Kessler has explained how in order to give them an architecturally suitable typographic background a special type was designed by Johnston and cut by Prince, and the book was then printed, page by page, by Craig and the Cranach Press in daily consultation. To this type Craig added a series of nineteen composition blocks, of which one example is included in this book (Plate 36). In a mysterious way, it leads us back to Serlio, to

FORTINBRAS · WOODCUT · 1927

the human figure in relation to its background, to the stillness of
true balance and proportion.

When the Cranach Press *Hamlet* appeared in English in September 1930, every copy was immediately sold. As well as being
one of the loveliest of books, it is a monument to the faithfulness
of Count Kessler, who first suggested the work early in 1912.

*

Craig has been an acknowledged leader of the Theatre in
Europe since 1911, the year a public banquet was held in his
honour in London when two hundred distinguished artists,
musicians and men of letters paid tribute to his work. Professor
William Rothenstein was in the chair and Ellen Terry was there,
delighting in her son's triumph. It was on this occasion that W.B.
Yeats made the cogent statement that 'a great age was an age that
employed its men of genius, and a poor age one that could not do
so. This age found it difficult to employ men of genius like Mr
Craig.' So it is hardly a surprise to find some correspondence in

26

The Saturday Review a dozen years later, urging that Craig should be given his rightful place in the English Theatre where he belongs, no support having been forthcoming for any of his ventures since his School had been swept away in the maelstrom of the 1914–18 war.

For in March 1913 Craig had opened his School for the Art of the Theatre in Florence. The Arena Goldoni, an open-air theatre with work-rooms, store-rooms and offices, used as a headquarters for publishing *The Mask* since 1908, was ideally suited for the purpose. The rent was only about a hundred pounds a year. Thirty students were enrolled and work hardly begun – there had only been three exhibitions of work done – when the war broke out, the students departed, funds from England ceased and the School had to be shut. Suddenly in 1916, the premises were requisitioned. There were five large model theatres in the school representing an outlay in work and materials of about £4000. Craig wrote to the British Embassy in Rome: 'The destruction of these models means the complete ruin of my career; they represent the visible exposition of my ideas on which depends my entire future'. Three months too late he was informed that he could remain on at the Arena Goldoni. But in the meantime it had been let by the proprietors to three different tenants and part to the military as a hospital, and the models had all been broken up by Craig. It became a barracks and was afterwards destroyed.

In *The Theatre Advancing* (1921) the reference to the School is succinct: 'It came in 1913; it went in 1914 ... for the war swept it away, and my supporter did not see the value of keeping the engine fires "banked". So the fires went out. It is a rare business, as you know, to relight the fires once they are allowed to go out.'

These particular fires were never lit again. Craig turned to theatrical research, to the writing of marionette plays, to the publication of *The Marionette* (1918), to restarting *The Mask*, which again flourished as a quarterly till 1929, and to much writing, including a delightful bit of autobiography in *Woodcuts and Some Words* (1924). In his authoritative introduction to the book Campbell Dodgson wrote:

Gifted, as a writer, with the courage of perennial youth; as a wood-engraver, with experience and taste acquired by five and twenty years of practice; as a reformer of the stage, with faith and hope, and even, to an appreciable degree, with charity, Mr Gordon Craig came well equipped to the task of which this volume is the achievement. ... My business here, I conceive, is to speak about Mr. Craig the wood-engraver. ... Notice the gradations produced by subtly varying the distances of line from line – their full charm will probably not survive the hand-printed proof – but notice especially the lovely line in the woodcuts that date from 1907, the period of the etchings for *Scene* (Plates 14, 17, 18). These have in spite of their small scale a monumental grandeur, and because of it an intimacy that yields ever fresh delight to the eye that returns again and again in quest of subtleties and felicities in the finish of this or that inch of the surface. After the quiescent and marmoreal beauties of these stately columns the eye turns with a new pleasure to the vivid play of flame and wind in the design that follows (Plate 19). ... I am thrilled by the light and shadow in *The Hour Glass* (Plate 24), pleased by the circles – not so much the obvious intersecting circles in the sky as the more ingenious and less apparent circles on the earth (Plate 15) and still more by the perspective of the tunnel-pergola which discloses, at the end of the intricate pleached alley, King Lear (Plate 16). ... The small, exquisite art that he has developed as his own is in perfect harmony and proportion with the little pieces of yellow polished boxwood that he loves. Is it not a great thing to achieve perfect proportion and harmony even in little?

28

It was in his essay 'The Artists of the Theatre of the Future', first published in *The Mask*, that Craig had written: 'Remember that on a sheet of paper which is but two inches square you can make a line which seems to tower in the air, and you can do the same on your stage, for it is all a matter of proportion and nothing to do with actuality.'

Denied a theatre, even a small one, and a troupe, even a limited one, to carry out his projects, Craig has shown them to us in another medium and on surfaces sometimes 'but two inches square'. It is all rather tragic, if it were not so comic, for ideas once let loose in the world run their course, following their own voli-tion – nothing can stop them, and the Theatre that Craig created for us was soon flourishing in Russia and Scandinavia, in Vienna, Berlin, Munich and Mannheim, in Budapest, Warsaw, Prague, Amsterdam and Tel Aviv, and to-day, with Jean-Louis Barrault, Decroux and others, in Paris.

His friends are legion and of every nationality, but he is feared and reviled by those who have failed to exploit him whom he calls 'the retro-aggressives, the thunder-stealers'. To these he shows his darker side. 'It's the joke I am enjoying more than a little,' he wrote to a friend not long ago when alluding to them; 'I've brought off the trick they dreaded and they don't even know how much they helped it.'

*

One more production Craig undertook, with the assistance of Johannes Poulsen: *The Crown Pretenders*, by Ibsen. It was for the jubilee of the Danish actors Adam and Johannes Poulsen at the Royal State Theatre, Copenhagen. You may read all about it in *A Production: 1926*, a book of monumental proportions published by the Oxford University Press in 1930 with many reproductions

29

in colour of his working drawings (Plates 39 and 40). That year also the King of Denmark decorated him with the Order of the Knights of the Dannebrog for his services to the Theatre.

Johannes Poulsen wrote of Craig:

> I have known the work of Gordon Craig for many years, but Gordon Craig himself I have only known for a few years. I find him one of the most charming and genial men that I have known. He is good and kind, like Hans Andersen; he is quite unselfish, like Tolstoy. He does not care a bit for money. His mind is that of a great philosopher. He can work himself to death for an idea; he can get out of his mind with rage, worse than any Italian nobleman, and after a moment he is as gentle as the blue sea on a summer's day. ... He has a sixth sense for that which is true, genuine and beautiful in art which is given to only a few persons in each century. As every judge of char-acter will understand from this, the fate of such a man is as always to be utilised by others to their profit and not his ... but while others have filled their own pockets, Gordon Craig has written his name in in-effaceable letters on the sky of the European mind.

CHRONOLOGY

Many incorrect statements having appeared about 'that legendary figure Gordon Craig', I wrote to him in Paris, asking for help in dating certain events correctly. He responded by sending me a small note-book crammed with information, from which I have extracted the following facts and dates.   J.L.

1872 Jan. 16. Was born at Stevenage, Herts., in Railway Street. Mother, Eleanor Alice. Father, Edward William.

1878 Mar. 28. E.T. as Olivia, Court Theatre. Dec. 28. As Ophelia, Lyceum Theatre.
   'Often at Hampton Court Palace.'

1881 Sees *Romeo and Juliet* at Lyceum – '*still remember the music and some scenes*'.

1882 Sees *Much Ado*, Lyceum – '*remember it all*'.

1883 Sees *Jane Eyre, Claudian*. E.T. and H.I.'s first visit to U.S.A.

1884 Sees Mary Anderson in *Ingomar. Twelfth Night*, Lyceum. E.T. and H.I.'s second visit to U.S.A. In Dec. is taken to America.

1885 Jan. 14. Appears as a gardener's boy in *Eugene Aram* in Chicago. *Faust* at Lyceum – '*remember it all*'.

1886 *Helena in Troas* at Hengler's Circus.
   Oct. 6. Edward William dies.

1889 Sept. 28. First night of *Dead Heart*, Lyceum. Engaged by H.I. at £5 a week to act a small part.
   Oct. Begins lessons in elocution with Mr Walter Lacy.

1890 Buys some books; Lewis' *Life of Goethe*, Tolstoy's *Kreutzer Sonata*; Henry Crabb Robinson's *Diary*, Marlowe's *Faustus*.
   May 27. Plays Moses in *Olivia* at Lyceum. On tour in summer months acts Biondello; Caleb Deecie in *Two Roses*, etc.

31

Sept. 20. First night of *Ravenswood*, Lyceum. Plays Henry
Ashton.

1891 Jan. 5. Plays Messenger and one of the Watch in *Much Ado
about Nothing*, Lyceum.

May 12. Plays Alexander Oldworthy with E.T. in *Nance Old-
field*, Lyceum.

June 2. Abel Quick in farce *A Regular Fix* by Morton, Lyceum.

Autumn – in many plays at Margate, Canterbury, etc. Plays
Charles Surface.

Oct. On tour with H.I. Plays Malcolm in *Macbeth*, Lorenzo in
Merchant of Venice, etc.

1892 Jan. 5. Plays Cromwell with H.I. in *Henry VIII*, Lyceum.

June. Hampton Court Palace: '*the fine rooms … the tall beds again*'.

Autumn at Margate Theatre acting Ford in *Merry Wives*,
Petruchio in *Taming of the Shrew*.

Nov. 10. Plays Oswald in *King Lear* with Irving at Lyceum.

1893 *The Echo*, London, gives him some sharp words for acting
Lorenzo badly at Lyceum.

Feb. Aubrey Beardsley makes drawing of E.G.C.

Buys *Essays of Montaigne* (Cotton trans.) and Callot's *Miseries of
War*.

Begins to watch a wood engraver at work; catches on like 'the
sedulous ape'.

Dec. At Uxbridge makes his first 'production', English translation of de Musset's *On ne badine pas avec l'amour*; acts Perdican –
Italia Conti, Camille.

1894 Seven months out of engagement.

Aug. 27. Joins a provincial company acting Romeo, Sept. 3.
Hamlet, Sept. 4 (at Hereford) Charles Surface, Cassio, Grati-
ano, etc. Tour lasts till Dec. 15.

Nov. 27 to 30. Reads *Robinson Crusoe* for first time – '*enchant-
ment*.'

1895 Jan. 12. *King Arthur* produced at Lyceum: he is no more in the
company.

Mar. 21. Joins Evelyn and Leigh Co. in *La Tosca*: plays Cavaradossi.

June. To Paisley to act all sorts in *New Magdalen*, *Streets of London*, Hamlet in *Hamlet*. James Pryde as Priest.

Aug. Dundee: *François Villon*. Aberdeen. Sept. Composing three or four songs – the music. Oct. some more songs. Nov. Out of work.

1896 Feb. 10. Joins Sarah Thorne Co. at Opera House, Chatham. Bargains for special parts at a flat rate of £2 a week playing Petruchio, the Corsican Brothers, Macbeth and Hamlet, with Benefit. His share of benefit reaches £4 : 6 : 2.

The Press announces that 'Mr C. is a splendid actor'. Craig's comment is: *'Suspect nothing left then but to retire from this splendid stage'*.

May 5. Rejoins Lyceum Co. at Liverpool, playing his old parts.

July. Prepares performance of *Romeo and Juliet* and *Hamlet* at Parkhurst Theatre: his own company.

Sept. 22. Plays Arviragus in *Cymbeline* with H.I. at Lyceum.

Dec. 19. Plays Edward IV with H.I. in *Richard III* at Lyceum.

1897 Jan. 18 to 23. His own company – Croydon.

Feb. 27. *Richard III* revived, plays Edward IV till April 7.

Comes to know Martin Shaw this year.

May 17. Acts Hamlet at Olympic Theatre: 6 nights and 2 matinees.

July. Plays Young Marlow in *She Stoops to Conquer*, with Granville Barker as Hastings, at Kingston-on-Thames.

End of year is end of his work under Irving.

1898 Begins publishing *The Page*.

1899 Publishes a Toy Book for children – *G.C. Book of Penny Toys* (20 large woodcuts and 23 decorations). Notice taken of *The Page*, vol. 2, in Belgium and in Italy. In London J.M. Bulloch, MacFall, Konody friendly to it.

To make something of a wretched living he draws for the newspapers and magazines. Makes sketches of Sarah Bernhardt,

Irving, Wyndham, Mr Foss, Harwood, Heslewood and others.

Publishes lithographs of Henry Irving and Ellen Terry (Lakeside Press).

1900 Publishes *Bookplates*, a booklet.

Beginning to design sceneries. 'Enter the Army' etc. (see *Towards a New Theatre*, 1913). Buys two books, Mantzius' *History of Theatrical Art*, vol. 1, and Vecellio's costume book *Degli abiti antichi*, 1589. 'Preparing to produce an opera.'

May 17, 18, 19. With Martin Shaw gives 3 performances of *Dido and Aeneas* by Purcell in Hampstead Conservatoire of Music for Purcell Operatic Society. The English Press cordial. £379 spent, about £378 taken. Had given some 6 months to preparing the work. M.F.S. and E.G.C. take no salary.

July. Already designing and rehearsing for Purcell's Masque from his opera *Dioclesian*.

1901 March 26. For one week M.F.S. and E.G.C. present *Dido and Aeneas* and the new attempt now called *The Masque of Love*, at Coronet Theatre, Notting Hill Gate, London. 8 months preparing for 6 days of performance.

A Souvenir Programme issued (14 engravings).

Balance sheet drawn up in November shows £533 : 6 : 4 received from the public, £534 : 6 : 8 expended on the work.

Publishes last volume of *The Page*.

1902 Since April preparing *Acis and Galatea*, by Handel and John Gay. On March 10 ring up the curtain at Great Queen Street Theatre, intending to perform to packed houses for 2 weeks. London Press both kindly and 'howling' (according to Graham Robertson).

'*The 15 Publics not sure of the way to Gt Queen Street Theatre or if "Acis" was English or Handel Dutch – or – or –. The piece was anyhow as good as we could make it. Some very wealthy men and one Cabinet Minister approached to do something – did nothing.*'

Publishes 'Souvenir Programme of *Acis and Galatea*' (9 col. plates, 10 half-tone plates).

Laurence Housman proposes M.F.S. and E.G.C. shall produce his play *Bethlehem*. Piece produced at the Imperial Institute in Dec.

1903 Jan. 31. Fred Terry produces *Sword and Song* at Shaftesbury Theatre and E.G.C. is given Act I, Scene 1 to deal with – and last act. Critics very friendly.

Ellen Terry decides to enter Theatrical Management with her children Edith and Edward Craig. She takes Imperial Theatre, Westminster. Ibsen's *The Vikings at Helgeland* selected as first piece to produce.

The Vikings produced April 15. Taken off May 9.

Much Ado about Nothing put on May 23. It runs a short time.

William Rothenstein letter to *Saturday Review*.

Support comes to E.G.C. – but not from London. Meantime he is designing and writing *Masque of Hunger*, *Masque of London* and *Masque of Lunatics*, begun in 1902.

July. He goes to Berlin to visit Dr Brahm of Lessing Theater. Arranges to do something there.

1904 Aug. He leaves for Berlin. Meets Count Kessler at Weimar. Prepares scene designs for Lessing Theater for *Venice Preserved* (Otway-Hofmannsthal) also making quantities of designs for plays and masques. Meets Isadora Duncan.

1905 Holds some dozen exhibitions in German cities and in Vienna. Makes many friends; none, except Count Kessler, will do anything to forward the theatre work. Writes small book *The Art of the Theatre*, with preface by Graham Robertson. It is published in German. Then in English (Foulis) and in Russian (pirated). Meantime full of project for publishing *The Mask*.

Venice Preserved produced at Lessing Theater, Berlin.

Designs and cuts 5 designs on wood for *The White Fan* (Hofmannsthal).

June. Reinhardt and assistants visit his studio to get a few ideas.

Oct. News comes of the death of Irving.

1906 Talk renewed of *The Mask*.

June. News of Ellen Terry Jubilee at Drury Lane Theatre reaches E.G.C. in Berlin.

Kathleen Bruce makes statuette of E.G.C.

Dutch edition of *The Art of the Theatre* appears with introductions by de Vos the actor, J. Baur the engraver and J. van Looy the painter.

Publishes *Isadora Duncan: Six Movement Designs* (Insel Verlag, Leipzig).

Oct. To Florence. First sight of Italy.

Preparing scene for *Rosmersholm* for Eleonora Duse.

Dec. 5. Performance of *Rosmersholm* at Pergola Theatre, Florence. Publishes *A Note on Rosmersholm*.

1907 This year *Screens*, *Über-Marionette* and *Black Figures* created and *The Mask* is slowly shaping.

The White Fan published by Insel Verlag, Leipzig.

Florence. 10 etchings made of SCENE.

Well awake to the confusion (and worse) of the English stage 2 years after Irving has died, E.G.C. writes *The Actor and the Über-Marionette* and *The Artists of the Theatre of the Future*.

1908 Exhibition of etchings for SCENE in London.

Publishes *A Portfolio of Etchings*. Cuts 19 more white (black) figures including 'Dancing Girl' and 'Hunger'.

March. *The Mask*, Vol. I. No. 1, at last and without financial support.

April 5. Leaves for St Petersburg.

Sept. Secures the Arena Goldoni as workshop-studio.

Oct. London. Solemn farce with Beerbohm Tree over a *Macbeth* production.

Florence. Puts *The Mask* into safe care of a Robber.

Nov. 1 to 25. Moscow. Agrees to produce *Hamlet* there.

1909 Recovers *The Mask* from the Robber. Extraordinary escape of the Robber. E.G.C. carves some 16 more white figures.

London. Makes another model stage for screens. E.T. brings
J.M. Barrie to see it, '*who* "*sees nothing there – yet all that was he
saw*"'.

These years he is steadily writing on serious stage problems day
by day and since 1907 has cut on boxwood some 119 designs.

Buys Moulton's *The Ancient Classical Drama* (1898) and Adolfo
Bartoli's *Scenari inediti* (Commedia dell'Arte).

1910 Jan. 1. London for one month. '*Indifference.*'

Feb. 1. Florence. Goes to Moscow, Feb. 28. Immediate work on
Hamlet. Room filled with large new model stage – daily re-
hearsal of scene by scene – with actors of each scene – reading
them the plan of action. Two stenographers, one English, one
Russian, taking down all that is said.

Designs and cuts many more figurines – 'Ghost' – 'Claudius' –
'Queen' – 'Sleeping King' – 'Poisoner' – 'Courtiers' seated ...
standing ... 'Musicians', etc. (Uses these later when designing
the Kessler *Hamlet*.)

May 7. Florence.

Aug. Milano. Makes four drawings for W.B. Yeats' *Plays for an
Irish Theatre* (see 1911), for *Deirdre* (1) *The Hour Glass* (1),
On Baile's Strand (2).

Carves 6 more white figures. Cuts 33 more boxwoods. Makes
some 30 to 40 sketches for *Hamlet* in Moscow.

1911 Jan. 12. In Dublin at Abbey Theatre, Yeats uses for first time
these new 'screens' in a play of his. (E.G.C. has given the poet
full rights – and a model stage and set of screens.)

June 19. To Paris.

July 5. London.

July 16. A Public Dinner is given in London in his honour.
200 friends present and Sir William (then Professor) Rothenstein in the chair. On Committee: Duchess of Sutherland,
Lady Gregory, Mrs Pat Campbell, Miss May Morris, Mrs
Rothenstein, W.B. Yeats, James Pryde, Augustus John,

Martin Shaw, Max Beerbohm, Charles Shannon, H.G. Wells, W. Strang, Roger Fry, Austin Harrison, Walter Crane, T. Sturge Moore, J. Martin Harvey, Laurence Binyon.

The Press active and generous.

Sept. Exhibition of designs for *Macbeth,* etc., at Leicester Galleries.

London. Daily showing on his large model stage the principles of the SCREENS.

Dec. In Moscow for *Hamlet* production – where he designs for Yeats The Blind Man in *On Baile's Strand.*

In London Heinemann issues *On the Art of the Theatre.* '*The press is generous as usual.*'

1912 Jan. 8. Répétition génerale of *Hamlet* in the Art Theatre. '*Complete success*' – ovations – speeches, etc.

Jan. 28. To Florence, leaving with Stanislavsky and Sulerjitsky innumerable ideas for the establishment of their school for the art of the theatre. It was opened in Moscow this same year and in it were two pupils of importance, Vakhtangov and Mlle Bierman.

In *The Mask* a significant half-page advertisement of a 'Hamlet' volume (see *Mask*, August 1908, Vol. I, Nos. 5 & 6). This is seen by Count Kessler who now – July 1912 – proposes to produce such a volume with E.G.C.

June. Paris. Preparing the woodcut designs for Count Kessler.

Sept. London. Exhibition of 95 drawings for the Moscow *Hamlet* at Leicester Galleries and 7 models for scenes.

Dec. While in Rome for 7 days' rest, sees Scarpetta of Naples acting.

1913 Jan. London again. *Towards a New Theatre* (Dent) appears.

A patron of the Arts agrees to support his studio-school for a year. This announced in London Press Feb. 27, E.T.'s birthday.

An International Theatre Exhibition held in Warsaw. E.G.C.'s Foreword to catalogue is printed in Polish and English.

Dec. Scarpelli visits Arena Goldoni at request of Giovanni Grasso – a genius of an actor – and sends report.

A Living Theatre issued from Florence describing the activities at the Arena.

1914 Feb. A large and important International Exhibition of Theatre work held in Zürich.

W.B. Yeats sails for U.S.A. and there delivers three lectures. One is on the theatre of Reinhardt and Gordon Craig.

April. In Naples and Pompeii. He writes there 'A Letter to John Semar, *The Theatre in Italy: Naples and Pompeii*', first published in *The Mask*.

June, July. In Florence a very large model in wood under construction for a projected performance of Bach's *St Matthew Passion*. The model is nearing completion when war is declared. No more funds for the work, all is closed down. Craig breaks up the model, preserving only a few of the smaller pieces – sort of keepsakes.

Craig comments – '*1915 to 1946 is a long game of patience – and for almost every artist on earth. Thirty years of breaking things up – has this been realised? Patience or impatience – laughing or fury, had to be the tune we played.*'

1915 *The Mask* appears as usual but has to mark time awhile in August.

1916 He now turns to the study of theatrical history. Writes some marionette plays: *School, The Gordian Knot, Once upon a time, The Tune the Old Cow died of, Fish and Bones* and others. Visits Pisa, Livorno, Bologna, Sabbioneta and its Teatro, Modena, Reggio, Parma and their ancient theatres. Decides to leave Florence and settle in Rome.

1917 Moves to Rapallo near Genoa.

1918 Preparing to republish *The Mask* again. Does so in April, volume 8.

Writes more puppet plays. Publishes *The Marionette*, Vol. I, 12 numbers.

November – Armistice. '*Very little to eat.*'

1919 *The Mask* again has to stop appearing after March number.

E.G.C.'s book *The Theatre Advancing* published in Boston, U.S.A.

Albert Rutherston's *Decoration in the Art of the Theatre* is published in London.

1920 London — *'pleasant but time entirely wasted'*. This in spite of friendly activity of Lovat Fraser and many artists.

Makes woodcut of 'Storm in King Lear'. *'A Critic praises it in "Observer". Nothing farcical in this ... big sales follow. Thank you, Konody.'*

Short visit to Paris where *On the Art of the Theatre* appears in a French translation.

1921 Rapallo. English edition of *The Theatre Advancing* (Constable, London) and *Puppets and Poets*, Chapbook (Poetry Bookshop, London) published.

1922 Invited by group of artists to open the International Exhibition of Theatre Art and Craft in Stedelijk Museum, Amsterdam. Frans Mijnssen, architect H.Th.Wijdeveld and F. Lensvelt the prime movers in this. It proves to be an important event in history of European Theatre.

He moves to have this same exhibition brought to England. It is opened first at Victoria and Albert Museum, South Kensington, June 3. The Exhibition passes to Manchester, Glasgow, Bradford with continued success through 1923 and is visited by over 350,000 people.

Count Kessler goes to Rapallo and the work on *Hamlet* begun in 1912 is resumed.

1923 Sept. *The Mask* reappears and this time as a single volume of 50 pages, volume 9.

E.G.C.'s *Scene* is issued by the Oxford University Press with a Foreword and Poem by John Masefield.

1924 Jan. *The Mask* as a quarterly reappears. It runs on regularly until end of 1929.

Feb. E.G.C.'s *Woodcuts and Some Words* issued by Dent and Sons, London, with a Foreword by Campbell Dodgson.

A Model for 'Storm Scene in King Lear' is made and sent to Wembley Exhibition.

Exhibition of woodcuts in London.

Italian edition of *On the Art of the Theatre* published.

1925 April. *Books and Theatres* accepted by Dent and Son.

May. Moves to Sturla near Genova.

Oct. E.G.C.'s *Nothing, or the Bookplate* issued by Chatto and Windus. Begins again to make several boxwood cuts.

1926 To Denmark to help Johannes and Adam Poulsen produce Ibsen's *The Crown Pretenders* in Copenhagen.

1927 '*There was an exhibition of all my wood-cuts held in Amsterdam this year. Arranged beautifully by H. Th. Wijdeveld. Catalogue designed by H. Th. W. with foreword by J. W. Buning. Poster by H. Kloopers, the actor artist. Altogether a charming affair thanks to my Dutch friends, who gave me no hint it was to be.*'

Oct. To Weimar, where the printing of *Hamlet* has begun. Printer, Mr Cole.

1928 June 26. Exhibition in London of E.G.C.'s designs for *The Crown Pretenders* is opened by Sir G. du Maurier.

Makes designs for a production of *Macbeth* for a Mr Tyler of America.

1929 To Weimar again where *Hamlet* is still being printed. He cuts several more blocks.

Sept. *The Mask* in difficulties. Decides to stop issuing it.

Dec. The German edition of *Hamlet* is now published by Cranach Press, Weimar: translation by Gerhart Hauptmann and woodcuts by E.G.C.

1930 Jan. 11. Berlin Exhibition of E.G.C.'s *Hamlet* designs at Gallery Flechtheim. Preface to the Catalogue by Count Kessler.

Aug. An article in *Les Nouvelles Littéraires*, Paris, by André Levinson on two books by E.G.C.

Sept. 25. First copy of E.G.C.'s book *Henry Irving* appears and is given a good reception by the press.

Sept. The English edition of *Hamlet*, Cranach Press, Weimar, appears, a reprint of the Second Quarto with 75 woodcuts by E.G.C.

*

This chronology has been compiled in the hope it will correct a number of loose statements and help to crystallize vague suppositions. The illustrations in this book cover the years 1900–30 so the Chronology ceases at the same date, but during the last seventeen years and indeed to-day Mr Craig is continually at work.

NOTES ON THE PLATES

1 BETHLEHEM. Young Shepherd. 1902.
   Production at the Imperial Institute, London, 1902.
2 ACIS AND GALATEA. Dress of Rushes. 1901.
   Production at the Great Queen Street Theatre, London, 1902.
3 MASQUE OF HUNGER. Prologue, 1904.
   'At the first note of music the curtain, which is a thing of shreds
   and patches, is rent in the middle, and a man with a hideous mask
   is seen standing on a little hillock of mud. He is breathing so heav-
   ily one might almost say he snorts: the kind of noise a bull makes
   when his mate has been removed to the shambles. From his right
   arm hangs a little, dead boy, which he stretches out to the audience.
   He shows this figure to all, moving it from right to left and from
   left to right, and all the time the sound of restrained bellowing is
   heard. His movements are slow and deliberate – we think that all
   emotion and all life has gone from him as well as from the dead
   figure which he holds. From every side, and beneath him, come
   the many echoes of his solitary cry, and these echoes take new
   shapes, resolving into the words "Pain ... Pain ... and Sorrow ..."
   which float singing in the air, or roll like billows around his feet.
   Then a black rain commences to fall, very softly at first, then like a
   hailstorm, and finally becomes so swift and dense that the two
   figures are lost to sight and everything ceases – sound, vision and
   all.' – *The Art of the Theatre* (1905).
4 ELECTRA. (Sophocles.) 1905.
   'I have never seen *Electra* acted, although I have seen the play
   done in a theatre. I saw it in Germany. Here my impression was
   that Electra was a little lady taking a little revenge with a lot
   of gusto. This impression was created because there was no beauty
   in the performance, and as no beauty, no Truth. "And what is
   Truth?" asks jesting Pilate. And Keats has answered him once
   and for all. Beauty is the complete, and even a touch of it here or

there in a performance showing that the performer has perceived the complete is enough to show us that the performer feels a true artist. If you are able to show that you have seen the complete completely, then you create a great work of art. This is not all said to prove anything, in favour of or against the design here, but perhaps there is the faintest glimmer in it of something which may be called beauty. I no longer have the eyes to find it there, although it is one of the designs that I like best to keep. What really is the best definition of beauty? It cannot be that which throws spirit and matter out of harmony! You cannot take sides: the two things must be fused before beauty can come near the place.' – *Towards a New Theatre* (1912).

5 MASQUE OF LONDON. Wapping Old Stairs, 1904.

'I remember it began somewhere in Persia or Arabia. In a great hall, flooded with light, a philosopher and a poet were discovered meditating (as they meditate in the East – not at all like a brown study) and the poet would not believe all the things which the philosopher was telling him of London, so he was shown that London is the place to which all the dead souls of men are brought and placed in some wretched case, either that of a newspaper boy or a shoeblack, given some trade, some papers to sell, some boots to black and sent along to his business. And I remember they all arrived in great barges down the brown Thames, and were shot out like sacks of coal and sent flying up those steps, their names or numbers being shouted out by some infernal spirit who stood ticking them off on a paper.' – *Towards a New Theatre* (1912).

6 DIDO AND ÆNEAS. Design for backcloth. Woodcut, 1900.
Production by the Purcell Operatic Society at Hampstead, 1900.

7 BETHLEHEM. From a photograph of the First Scene in Laurence Housman's play produced at the Imperial Institute, South Kensington, December 1902.

8 SWORD AND SONG. Act 3. Woodcut, 1903.
Production at the Shaftesbury Theatre, London, 1903.

'It was done to guide the scene-painter. I had not my own painting room or I should have been my own scene-painter.'

9 THE VIKINGS (Ibsen). Woodcut, 1908.
Production at Imperial Theatre, Westminster, 1903.
'I made some fifty or so drawings and some hundred sketches,
working, as the theatre-folk in those days had to work, all day and
nearly all night, for months, rehearsing a charming company, who
acted so well that everyone remembers their performances; my
mise en scène is forgotten, I think. It was praised by a few, patron-
ised by a few more, and allowed to drift out of the English theatre.
So I take it I was a little before my time, a very careless thing to be;
after this I was out of work for many months.' – *Woodcuts and Some
Words* (1924).

10 VENICE PRESERVED (Otway). Act II. The Conspirators.
1904.
Production at the Lessing Theater, Berlin, 1905.
'This had a dappled dark blue sky.'

11 VENICE PRESERVED. Another design for Act II, 1904.
'I would not propose such a scene for any theatre except one of a
special form – that is to say, with the seats all on an inclined floor.'

12 PSYCHE. Project for a ballet, 1907.
'This represents the moment when Psyche in the house is "beset
with doubts and fears".'

13 MACBETH. Act II. Project, 1908.

14 Design for scene: In Italy. Woodcut, 1907.
'How doth the city sit solitary that was full of people!'

15 Design for stage scene. Woodcut, 1908.

16 For *King Lear*. Woodcut, 1908.

17 SCENE. Woodcut, 1908.

18 Design for stage scene. Woodcut, 1907.

19 Troy burning. Woodcut, 1908.

20 SCENE: Small opening. Etching, 1907.
The opening or beginning of the series of rapid moving glimpses
of SCENE.

A form simple and austere ascends with prolonged patience like the awakening of a thought in a dream. A second and a third form seem to follow. … Always a double birth repeating … a fourth, a fifth, a seventh, and yet as we look we seem to see but four … that first form which gave birth has passed; those two forms to which it gave birth have passed. … For the fulfilment of this most superb dream must first come the union of the three Arts … Architecture, Music and Motion.' – From the Preface to the Portfolio of Etchings, published in *The Mask*, December 1908.

21 SCENE: Little Temple. Etching, 1911.
'The last etching and the last moment of SCENE.'

22 ON BAILE'S STRAND (W.B. Yeats). The Blind Man. Etching, 1911.
Production at the Abbey Theatre, Dublin, 1911.
'This is a design for a mask. It is rather more realistic than a mask should be, but as a beginning I dare say it will do. The eyes are closed, they are still cross, and I take it that the man sees with his nose. I imagine that he smells his way in the dark, and he seems to keep up an eternal kind of windy whistling with his pursed-up lips. The advantage of a mask over a face is that it is always repeating unerringly the poetic fancy, repeating on Monday in 1912 exactly what it said on Saturday in 1909 and what it will say on Wednesday in 1999. Durability was the dominant idea in Egyptian art. The theatre must learn that lesson. "But," you say, "the actor does not live for ever, he is not immortal." Exactly, my friends, but his mask can live for ever. Let us again cover his face with a mask in order that his expression – the visualised expression of the Poetic spirit – shall be everlasting.'

23 THE HOUR GLASS (W.B. Yeats). Mask of the Fool. Woodcut, 1911.
Production at the Abbey Theatre, Dublin, 1911.

24 THE HOUR GLASS (W.B. Yeats). Woodcut, 1911.
'I called it *The Hourglass* because it wasn't *unlike* – but strictly not

like. Compare it with the drawing in Yeats' volume of *Plays for a Irish Theatre. That* is precise.'

25 MODEL STAGE. Setting for a scene in *Hamlet*.
Production at the Moscow Art Theatre, January 1912.

BLACK FIGURES

PRINTS TAKEN FROM MARIONETTES

26 MERCHANT OF VENICE. Young Gobbo, 1909.
27 MERCHANT OF VENICE. Old Gobbo, 1909.

DESIGNS USED
IN THE TWO CRANACH PRESS EDITIONS OF 'HAMLET'
PREPARED BY COUNT KESSLER, WEIMAR

28 Hamlet and Daemon, 1909.
29 Second Gravedigger, 1913.
30 Ghost, 1912.
31 An Actor, 1912.
32 'The actors are come hither', 1927.
33 Hamlet greeting the actors, 1927.
34 Player-King asleep in the orchard, 1927.
35 'Lights, lights, lights!' 1927.
36 Composition block.

*

37 MACBETH. Act I, Scene 2. A camp near Forres, 1928.
Production at the Knickerbocker Theatre, New York, 1928.
38 MACBETH. Act I, Scene 3, 1928.
'So foul and fair a day I have not seen.'
Production at the Knickerbocker Theatre, New York, 1928.
39 THE CROWN PRETENDERS (Ibsen). Act I, Scene 1. 1926.
Production at the Royal Theatre, Copenhagen, 1926.
'We planted these four small scenes, consisting of practically
nothing solid, on this stage structure. The church pillars which

you see were projected: and when I saw them projected for the first time, I was satisfied. I had never used any projection by light on a grand scale until then, although I had done many hundreds on a little model stage of my own, in Florence, Rome and in Rapallo. But when I saw this projection on the vast Copenhagen stage – this church projected through the elaborate machines of Mr Neilsen from a little plate which measured three inches square, I felt not only very grateful to Mr Neilsen but also to the great Adolf Linnebach, that Bibiena of the modern stage, who for the last thirty years or more has created marvellous inventions to help craftsmen of the theatre. Very often the mere machinist, without genius, doesn't help the artist though undoubtedly he tries to, but Linnebach has helped enormously.' – *A Production: 1926* (1930).

40 THE CROWN PRETENDERS (Ibsen). Act II. Banqueting Scene. 1926. Production at the Royal Theatre, Copenhagen, 1926.

*

ACKNOWLEDGMENTS

The author and editor wish to express their gratitude to Mr Gordon Craig without whose help this book would not have been possible. They wish to thank him in particular for the loan of catalogues, books and photos as well as original drawings and woodcuts and for permission to reproduce them. Their thanks are also due to Mr Edward Carrick and Mr Robert Donat for the loan of original drawings reproduced on Plates 4 and 5.

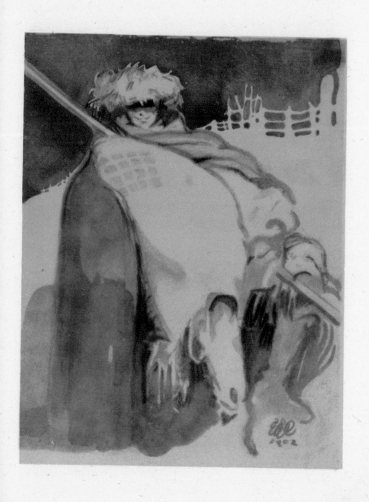

Bethlehem: Young Shepherd. 1902

Acis and Galatea: Dress of Rushes. 1901.

HUNGER.

The Masque of Hunger. 1904

Electra. 1905

The Masque of London: Wapping Old Stairs. 1904

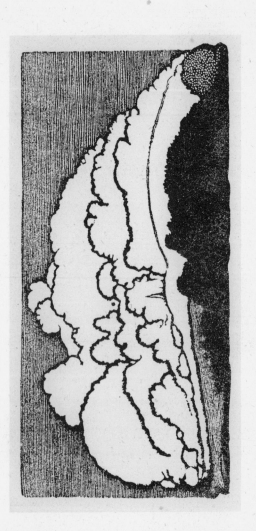

Dido and Aeneas : Backcloth. 1900

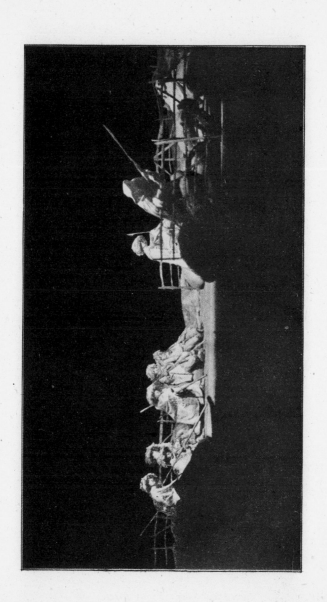

Bethlehem: First Scene. From a photograph taken during rehearsals. 1902

Sword and Song : Forest Trees. 1903

The Vikings (Ibsen). 1908

Venice Preserved : (Otway) Act II. The Conspirators. 1904

Venice Preserved : The Conspirators.   Another design.   1904

Psyche: Project for Ballet. 1907

Macbeth : Act II. 1908

In Italy: Design for a Scene. 1907

Design for Stage Scene. 1908

King Lear. 1908

SCENE 1908

Design for Stage Scene. 1907

Troy Burning. 1908

SCENE *Small Opening.* 1907

SCENE *The Temple.* 1911

22

On Baile's Strand (Yeats): The Blind Man. 1911

The Hour Glass (Yeats) : Mask of the Fool. 1911

The Hour Glass (Yeats): Scene. 1911

Photograph of a model stage setting for a scene in Hamlet.   1912

Merchant of Venice : Young Gobbo. 1909

Merchant of Venice : Old Gobbo. 1909

Hamlet: Hamlet and Daemon. 1909

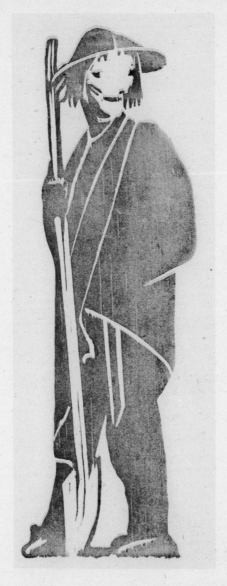

Hamlet : Second Grave-Digger. 1913

Hamlet : Ghost. 1912

Hamlet : An Actor. 1912

Hamlet : The Actors

Hamlet : Hamlet greeting the Actors

Hamlet : Player-King asleep in the Orchard. 1927

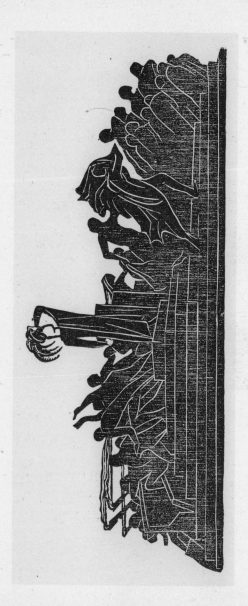

Hamlet : " Lights, Lights, Lights." 1927

Hamlet: Composition block

Macbeth : Act I, Scene 2. 1928

Macbeth: Act I, Scene 3. 1928

The Crown Pretenders (Ibsen) : Act I, Scene I, 1926

The Crown Pretenders (Ibsen): Act II. 1926